Electra by Euripides

Translated from the Greek by E.P. Coleridge

Euripides is rightly lauded as one of the great dramatists of all time. In his lifetime, he wrote over 90 plays and although only 18 have survived they reveal the scope and reach of his genius.

Euripides is identified with many theatrical innovations that have influenced drama all the way down to modern times, especially in the representation of traditional, mythical heroes as ordinary people in extraordinary circumstances.

As would be expected from a life lived 2,500 years ago, details of it are few and far between. Accounts of his life, written down the ages, do exist but whether much is reliable or surmised is open to debate.

Most accounts agree that he was born on Salamis Island around 480 BC, to mother Cleito and father Mnesarchus, a retailer who lived in a village near Athens. Upon the receipt of an oracle saying that his son was fated to win "crowns of victory", Mnesarchus insisted that the boy should train for a career in athletics.

However, what is clear is that athletics was not to be the way to win crowns of victory. Euripides had been lucky enough to have been born in the era as the other two masters of Greek Tragedy; Sophocles and Æschylus. It was in their footsteps that he was destined to follow.

His first play was performed some thirteen years after the first of Socrates plays and a mere three years after Æschylus had written his classic The Oristria.

Theatre was becoming a very important part of the Greek culture. The Dionysia, held annually, was the most important festival of theatre and second only to the fore-runner of the Olympic games, the Panathenia, held every four years, in appeal.

Euripides first competed in the City Dionysia, in 455 BC, one year after the death of Æschylus, and, incredibly, it was not until 441 BC that he won first prize. His final competition in Athens was in 408 BC. The Bacchae and Iphigenia in Aulis were performed after his death in 405 BC and first prize was awarded posthumously. Altogether his plays won first prize only five times.

Euripides was also a great lyric poet. In Medea, for example, he composed for his city, Athens, "the noblest of her songs of praise". His lyric skills however are not just confined to individual poems: "A play of Euripides is a musical whole....one song echoes motifs from the preceding song, while introducing new ones."

Much of his life and his whole career coincided with the struggle between Athens and Sparta for hegemony in Greece but he didn't live to see the final defeat of his city.

Euripides fell out of favour with his fellow Athenian citizens and retired to the court of Archelaus, king of Macedon, who treated him with consideration and affection.

At his death, in around 406BC, he was mourned by the king, who, refusing the request of the Athenians that his remains be carried back to the Greek city, buried him with much splendor within his own dominions. His tomb was placed at the confluence of two streams, near Arethusa in Macedonia, and a cenotaph was built to his memory on the road from Athens towards the Piraeus.

Index of Contents

THE PERSONS

A PEASANT OF MYCENAE, husband of ELECTRA
ELECTRA, daughter of Agamemnon
ORESTES, son of Agamemnon
PYLADES, friend Of ORESTES
CHORUS OF ARGIVE COUNTRY-WOMEN
CLYTEMNESTRA, widow of Agamemnon
OLD MAN, formerly servant of Agamemnon
MESSENGER
THE DIOSCURI

SCENE

Before the hut of the Peasant, in the country on the borders of Argolis.

ELECTRA

It is just before sunrise. The **PEASANT** is discovered alone.

PEASANT
O Argos, ancient land, and streams of Inachus, whence on a day king Agamemnon sailed to the realm of Troy, carrying his warriors aboard a thousand ships; and after he had slain Priam who was reigning in Ilium and captured the famous city of Dardanus, he came hither to Argos and has set up high on the temple-walls many a trophy, spoil of the barbarians. Though all went well with him in Troy, yet was he slain in his own palace by the guile of his wife Clytemnestra and the hand of Aegisthus, son of Thyestes. So he died and left behind him the ancient sceptre of Tantalus, and Aegisthus reigns in his stead, with the daughter of Tyndareus, Agamemnon's queen, to wife. Now as for those whom he left in his halls, when he sailed to Troy, his son Orestes and his tender daughter Electra,the boy Orestes, as he was like

to be slain by Aegisthus, his sire's old foster-father secretly removed to the land of Phocis and gave to Strophius to bring up, but the maid Electra abode in her father's house, and soon as she had budded into maidenhood, came all the princes of Hellas asking her hand in marriage. But Aegisthus kept her at home for fear she might bear a son to some chieftain who would avenge Agamemnon, nor would he betroth her unto any. But when e'en thus there seemed some room for fear that she might bear some noble lord a child by stealth and Aegisthus was minded to slay her, her mother, though she had a cruel heart, yet rescued the maiden from his hand. For she could find excuses for having slain her husband, but she feared the hatred she would incur for her children's murder. Wherefore Aegisthus devised this scheme; on Agamemnon's son who had escaped his realm by flight he set a price to be paid to any who should slay him, while he gave Electra to me in marriage, whose ancestors were citizens of Mycenae. It is not that I blame myself for; my family was noble enough, though certainly impoverished, and so my good birth suffers. By making for her this weak alliance he thought he would have little to fear. For if some man of high position had married her, he might have revived the vengeance for Agamemnon's murder, which now is sleeping; in which case Aegisthus would have paid the penalty. But Cypris is my witness that I have ever respected her maidenhood; she is still as though unwed. Unworthy as I am, honour forbids that I should so affront the daughter of a better man. Yea, and I am sorry for Orestes, hapless youth, who is called my kinsman, to think that he should ever return to Argos and behold his sister's wretched marriage. And whoso counts me but a fool for leaving a tender maid untouched when I have her in my house, to him I say, he measures purity by the vicious standard of his own soul, a standard like himself.

[**ELECTRA** enters from the hut, carrying a water pitcher on her head. She is meanly clad.]

ELECTRA
O sable night, nurse of the golden stars! beneath thy pall I go to fetch water from the brook with my pitcher poised upon my head, not indeed because I am forced to this necessity, but that to the gods I may display the affronts Aegisthus puts upon me, and to the wide firmament pour out my lamentation for my sire. For my own mother, the baleful daughter of Tyndareus, hath cast me forth from her house to gratify her lord; for since she hath borne other children to Aegisthus she puts me and Orestes on one side at home.

PEASANT
Oh! why, poor maiden, dost thou toil so hard on my behalf, thou that aforetime wert reared so daintily? why canst thou not forego thy labour, as I bid thee?

ELECTRA
As a god's I count thy kindness to me, for in my distress thou hast never made a mock at me. 'Tis rare fortune when mortals find such healing balm for their cruel wounds as 'tis my lot to find in thee. Wherefore I ought, though thou forbid me, to lighten thy labours, as far as my strength allows, and share all burdens with thee to ease thy load. Thou hast enough to do abroad; 'tis only right that I should keep thy house in order. For when the toiler cometh to his home from the field, it is pleasant to find all comfortable in the house.

PEASANT
If such thy pleasure, go thy way; for, after all, the spring is no great distance from my house. And at break of day I will drive my steers to my glebe and sow my crop. For no idler, though he has the gods' names ever on his lips, can gather a livelihood without hard work.

[ELECTRA and the PEASANT go out. A moment later ORESTES and PYLADES enter.]

ORESTES
Ah Pylades, I put thee first 'mongst men for thy love, thy loyalty and friendliness to me; for thou alone of all my friends wouldst still honour poor Orestes, in spite of the grievous plight whereto I am reduced by Aegisthus, who with my accursed mother's aid slew my sire. I am come from Apollo's mystic shrine to the soil of Argos, without the knowledge of any, to avenge my father's death upon his murderers. Last night went unto his tomb and wept thereon, cutting off my hair as an offering and pouring o'er the grave the blood of a sheep for sacrifice, unmarked by those who lord it o'er this land. And now though I enter not the walled town, yet by coming to the borders of the land I combine two objects; I can escape to another country if any spy me out and recognize me, and at the same time seek my sister, for I am told she is a maid no longer but is married and living here, that I may meet her, and, after enlisting her aid in the deed of blood, learn for certain what is happening in the town. Let us now, since dawn is uplifting her radiant eye, step aside from this path. For maybe some labouring man or serving maid will come in sight, of whom we may inquire whether it is here that my sister hath her home. Lo! yonder I see a servant bearing a full pitcher of water on her shaven head; let us sit down and make inquiry of this bond-maid, if haply we may glean some tidings of the matter which brought us hither, Pylades.

[They retire a little, as ELECTRA returns from the spring.]

ELECTRA [chanting, strophe 1]
Bestir thy lagging feet, 'tis high time; on, on o'er thy path of tears! ah misery! I am Agamemnon's daughter, she whom Clytemnestra, hateful child of Tyndareus, bare; hapless Electra is the name my countrymen call me. Ah me! for my cruel lot, my hateful existence! O my father Agamemnon! in Hades art thou laid, butchered by thy wife and Aegisthus. Come, raise with me that dirge once more; uplift the woful strain that brings relief.

[antistrophe 1]

On, on o'er thy path of tears! ah misery! And thou, poor brother, in what city and house art thou a slave, leaving thy suffering sister behind in the halls of our fathers to drain the cup of bitterness? Oh! come, great Zeus, to set me free from this life of sorrow, and to avenge my sire in the blood of his foes, bringing the wanderer home to Argos.

[strophe 2]

Take this pitcher from my head, put it down, that I may wake betimes, while it is yet night, my lamentation for my sire, my doleful chant, my dirge of death, for thee, my father in thy grave, which day by day I do rehearse, rending my skin with my nails, and smiting on my shaven head in mourning for thy death. Woe, woe! rend the cheek; like a swan with clear loud note beside the brimming river calling to its parent dear that lies a-dying in the meshes of the crafty net, so I bewail thee, my hapless sire,

[antistrophe 2]

After that last fatal bath of thine laid out most piteously in death. Oh! the horror of that axe which hacked thee so cruelly, my sire! oh! the bitter thought that prompted thy return from Troy! With no garlands or victor's crowns did thy wife welcome thee, but with his two-edged sword she made thee the sad sport of Aegisthus and kept her treacherous paramour.

[The **CHORUS OF ARGIVE COUNTRY-WOMEN** enter. The following lines between **ELECTRA** and the **CHORUS** are sung responsively.]

CHORUS [strophe]
O Electra, daughter of Agamemnon, to thy rustic cot I come, for a messenger hath arrived, a highlander from Mycenae, one who lives on milk, announcing that the Argives are proclaiming a sacrifice for the third day from now, and all our maidens are to go to Hera's temple.

ELECTRA
Kind friends, my heart is not set on festivity, nor do necklaces of gold cause any flutter in my sorrowing bosom, nor will I stand up with the maidens of Argos to beat my foot in the mazy dance. Tears have been my meat day and night; ah misery! See my unkempt hair, my tattered dress; are they fit for a princess, a daughter of Agamemnon, or for Troy which once thought of my father as its captor?

CHORUS [antistrophe]
Mighty is the goddess; so come, and borrow of me broidered robes for apparel and jewels of gold that add a further grace to beauty's charms. Dost think to triumph o'er thy foes by tears, if thou honour not the gods? 'Tis not by lamentation but by pious prayers to heaved that thou, my daughter, wilt make fortune smile on thee.

ELECTRA
No god hearkens to the voice of lost Electra, or heeds the sacrifices offered by my father long ago. Ah woe for the dead! woe for the living wanderer, who dwelleth in some foreign land, an outcast and vagabond at a menial board, sprung though he is of a famous sire! Myself, too, in a poor man's hut do dwell, wasting my soul with grief, an exile from my father's halls, here by the scarred hill-side; while my mother is wedded to a new husband in a marriage stained by blood.

LEADER OF THE CHORUS
Many a woe to Hellas and thy house did Helen, thy mother's sister, cause.

ELECTRA [catching sight of **ORESTES** and **PYLADES**]
Ha! Friends, I break off my lament; yonder are strangers just leaving the place of ambush where they were couching, and making for the house. We must seek to escape the villains by flying, thou along the path and I into my cottage.

ORESTES
Stay, poor maid; fear no violence from me.

ELECTRA
O Phoebus Apollo I beseech thee spare my life.

ORESTES
Give me the lives of others more my foes than thou!

ELECTRA
Begone! touch me not! thou hast no right to.

ORESTES

There is none I have a better right to touch.

ELECTRA

How is it then thou waylayest me, sword in hand, near my house?

ORESTES

Wait and hear, and thou wilt soon agree with me

ELECTRA

Here I stand; I am in thy power in any case, since thou art the stronger.

ORESTES

I am come to thee with news of thy brother.

ELECTRA

O best of friends! is he alive or dead?

ORESTES

Alive; I would fain give thee my good news first.

ELECTRA

God bless thee! in return for thy welcome tidings.

ORESTES

I am prepared to share that blessing between us.

ELECTRA

In what land is my poor brother spending his dreary exile?

ORESTES

His ruined life does not conform to the customs of any one city.

ELECTRA

Surely he does not want for daily bread?

ORESTES

Bread he has, but an exile is a helpless man at best.

ELECTRA

What is this message thou hast brought from him?

ORESTES

He asks, "Art thou alive? and if so, How art thou faring?"

ELECTRA

Well, first thou seest how haggard I am grown.

ORESTES
So wasted with sorrow that I weep for thee.

ELECTRA
Next mark my head, shorn and shaven like a Scythian's.

ORESTES
Thy brother's fate and father's death no doubt disturb thee.

ELECTRA
Yes, alas! for what have I more dear than these?

ORESTES
Ah! and what dost thou suppose is dearer to thy brother?

ELECTRA
He is far away, not here to show his love to me.

ORESTES
Wherefore art thou living here far from the city?

ELECTRA
I am wedded, sir; a fatal match!

ORESTES
Alas! for thy brother; I pity him. Is thy husband of Mycenae?

ELECTRA
He is not the man to whom my father ever thought of betrothing me.

ORESTES
Tell me all, that I may report it to thy brother.

ELECTRA
I live apart from my husband in this house.

ORESTES
The only fit inmate would be a hind or herd.

ELECTRA
Poor he is, yet he displays a generous consideration for me.

ORESTES
Why, what is this consideration that attaches to thy husband?

ELECTRA
He has never presumed to claim from me a husband's rights.

ORESTES

Is he under a vow of chastity? or does he disdain thee?

ELECTRA

He thought he had no right to flout my ancestry.

ORESTES

How was it he was not overjoyed at winning such a bride?

ELECTRA

He does not recognize the right of him who disposed of my hand.

ORESTES

I understand; he was afraid of the vengeance of Orestes hereafter.

ELECTRA

There was that fear, but he was a virtuous man as well.

ORESTES

Ah! a noble nature this! He deserves kind treatment.

ELECTRA

Yes, if ever the wanderer return.

ORESTES

But did thy own mother give in to this?

ELECTRA

'Tis her husband, not her children that a woman loves, sir stranger.

ORESTES

Wherefore did Aegisthus put this affront on thee?

ELECTRA

His design in giving me to such a husband was to weaken my offspring

ORESTES

To prevent thee bearing sons, I suppose, who should punish him?

ELECTRA

That was his plan; God grant I may avenge me on him for it!

ORESTES

Does thy mother's husband know that thou art yet a maid?

ELECTRA

He does not; our silence robs him of that knowledge.

ORESTES
Are these women friends of thine, who overhear our talk?

ELECTRA
They are, and they will keep our conversation perfectly secret.

ORESTES
What could Orestes do in this matter, if he did return?

ELECTRA
Canst thou ask? Shame on thee for that! Is not this the time for action?

ORESTES
But suppose he comes, how could he slay his father's murderers?

ELECTRA
By boldly meting out the same fate that his father had meted out to him by his foes.

ORESTES
Wouldst thou be brave enough to help him slay his mother?

ELECTRA
Aye, with the self-same axe that drank my father's blood.

ORESTES
Am I to tell him this, and that thy purpose firmly holds?

ELECTRA
Once I have shed my mother's blood o'er his, then welcome death!

ORESTES
Ah! would Orestes were standing near to hear that!

ELECTRA I should not know him, sir, if I saw him.

ORESTES
No wonder; you were both children when you parted.

ELECTRA
There is only one of my friends would recognize him.

ORESTES
The man maybe who is said to have snatched him away from being murdered?

ELECTRA
Yes, the old servant who tended my father's childhood long ago.

ORESTES

Did thy father's corpse obtain burial?

ELECTRA
Such burial as it was, after his body had been flung forth from the palace.

ORESTES
O God! how awful is thy story! Yes, there is a feeling, arising even from another's distress, that wrings the human heart. Say on, that when know the loveless tale, which yet I needs must hear, I may carry it to thy brother. For pity, though it has no place in ignorant natures, is inborn in the wise; still it may cause trouble to find excessive cleverness amongst the wise.

LEADER
I too am stirred by the same desire as the stranger. For dwelling so far from the city I know nothing of its ills, and I should like to hear about them now myself.

ELECTRA
I will tell you, if I may; and surely I may tell a friend about my own and my father's grievous misfortunes. Now since thou movest me to speak, I entreat thee, sir, tell Orestes of our sorrows; first, describe the dress I wear, the load of squalor that oppresses me, the hovel I inhabit after my royal home; tell him how hard I have to work at weaving clothes myself or else go barely clad and do without; how I carry home on my head water from the brook; no part have I in holy festival, no place amid the dance; a maiden still I turn from married dames and from Castor too, to whom they betrothed me before he joined the heavenly host, for I was his kinswoman. Meantime my mother, 'mid the spoils of Troy, is seated on her throne, and at her foot-stool slaves from Asia stand and wait, captives of my father's spear, whose Trojan robes are fastened with brooches of gold. And there on the wall my father's blood still leaves a deep dark stain, while his murderer mounts the dead man's car and fareth forth, proudly grasping in his blood-stained hands the sceptre with which Agamemnon would marshal the sons of Hellas. Dishonoured lies his grave; naught as yet hath it received of drink outpoured or myrtle-spray, but bare of ornament his tomb is left. Yea, and 'tis said that noble hero who is wedded to my mother, in his drunken fits, doth leap upon the grave, and pelt with stones my father's monument, boldly gibing at us on this wise, "Where is thy son Orestes? Is he ever coming in his glory to defend thy tomb?" Thus is Orestes flouted behind his back. Oh! tell him this, kind sir, I pray thee. And there be many calling him to come,—I am but their mouthpiece,—these suppliant hands, this tongue, my broken heart, my shaven head, and his own father too. For 'tis shameful that the sire should have destroyed Troy's race and the son yet prove too weak to pit himself against one foe unto the death, albeit he has youth and better blood as well.

LEADER
Lo! here is thy husband hurrying homeward, his labour done.

PEASANT [entering and catching sight of strangers talking to **ELECTRA**]
Ha! who are these strangers I see at my door? And why are they come hither to my rustic gate? can they want my help? for 'tis unseemly for a woman to stand talking with young men.

ELECTRA
Dear husband, be not suspicious of me. For thou shalt hear the truth; these strangers have come to bring me news of Orestes. Good sirs, pardon him those words.

PEASANT

What say they? is that hero yet alive and in the light of day?

He is; at least they say so, and I believe them.

PEASANT

Surely then he hath some memory of his father and thy wrongs?

ELECTRA

These are things to hope for; a man in exile is helpless.

PEASANT

What message have they brought from Orestes?

ELECTRA

He sent them to spy out my evil case.

PEASANT

Well, they only see a part of it, though maybe thou art telling them the rest.

ELECTRA

They know all; there is nothing further they need ask.

PEASANT

Long ere this then shouldst thou have thrown open our doors to them. Enter, sirs; for in return for your good tidings, shall ye find such cheer as my house affords. Ho! servants, take their baggage within; make no excuses, for ye are friends sent by one I love; and poor though I am, yet will I never show meanness in my habits.

ORESTES

'Fore heaven! is this the man who is helping thee to frustrate thy marriage, because he will not shame Orestes?

ELECTRA

This is he whom they call my husband, woe is me!

ORESTES

Ah! there is no sure mark to recognize a man's worth; for human nature hath in it an element of confusion. For I have seen ere now the son of noble sire prove himself a worthless knave, and virtuous children sprung from evil parents; likewise dearth in a rich man's spirit, and in a poor man's frame a mighty soul. By what standard then shall we rightly judge these things? By wealth? An evil test to use. By poverty then? Nay, poverty suffers from this, that it teaches a man to play the villain from necessity. To martial prowess must I turn? But who could pronounce who is the valiant man merely from the look of his spear? Better is it to leave these matters to themselves without troubling. For here is a man of no account in Argos, with no family reputation to boast, one of the common herd, proved a very hero. A truce to your folly! ye self-deceivers, swollen with idle fancies; learn to judge men by their converse, and by their habits decide who are noble. Such are they who rule aright both states and families; while those forms of flesh, devoid of intellect, are but figure-heads in the market-place. The strong arm, again, no more than the weak awaits the battle-shock, for this depends on natural courage. Well! absent or present, Agamemnon's son, whose business brings us here, deserves this of us, so let us accept a lodging in this house. [Calling to his **SERVANTS**] Ho! sirrahs, go within. A humble host, who does his best, in preference to a wealthy man for me! And so I thankfully accept this peasant's proffered welcome, though I could have preferred that thy brother were conducting me to share his fortune in his halls. Maybe he yet will come; for the oracles of Loxias are sure, but to man's divining "Farewell" say I.

[**ORESTES**, **PYLADES** and their **ATTENDANTS** go into the hut.]

LEADER
Electra, I feel a warmer glow of joy suffuse my heart than ever heretofore; perchance our fortune, moving on at last, will find a happy resting-place.

ELECTRA
O reckless man, why didst thou welcome strangers like these, so far beyond thy station, knowing the poverty of thy house?

PEASANT
Why? if they are really as noble as they seem, surely they will be equally content with rich or humble fare.

ELECTRA
Well. since thou hast made this error, poor man as thou art, go to my father's kind old foster-sire; on the bank of the river Tanaus, the boundary 'twixt Argos and the land of Sparta, he tends his flocks, an outcast from the city; bid him come hither to our house and some provision for the strangers' entertainment. Glad will he be, and will offer thanks to heaven to hear that the child, whom once he saved, is yet alive. I shall get nothing from my mother from my ancestral halls; for we should rue our message, were she to learn, unnatural wretch! that Orestes liveth.

PEASANT
I will take this message to the old man, if it seem good to thee; but get thee in at once and there make ready. A woman, when she chooses, can find dainties in plenty to garnish a feast. Besides, there is quite enough in the house to satisfy them with food for one day at least. 'Tis in such cases, when I come to muse thereon, that I discern the mighty power of wealth, whether to give to strangers, or to expend in curing the body when it falls sick; but our daily food is a small matter; for all of us, rich as well as poor, are in like case, as soon as we are satisfied.

[The **PEASANT** departs as **ELECTRA** enters the hut.]

CHORUS [singing, strophe 1]
Ye famous ships, that on a day were brought to land at Troy by those countless oars, what time ye led the Nereids' dance, where the dolphin music-loving rolled and gambolled round your dusky prows, escorting Achilles, nimble son of Thetis, when he went with Agamemnon to the banks of Trojan Simois;

[antistrophe 1]

When Nereids left Euboea's strand, bringing from Hephaestus' golden forge the harness he had fashioned for that warrior's use; him long they sought o'er Pelion and Ossa's spurs, ranging the sacred glens and the peaks of Nymphaea, where his knightly sire was training up a light for Hellas, even the sea-born son of Thetis, a warrior swift to help the sons of Atreus.

[strophe 2]

One that came from Ilium, and set foot in the haven of Nauplia, told me that on the circle of thy far-famed targe, O son of Thetis, was wrought this blazon, a terror to the Phrygians; on the rim of the buckler Perseus with winged sandals, was bearing in his hand across the main the Gorgon's head, just severed by the aid of Hermes, the messenger of Zeus, that rural god whom Maia bore;

[antistrophe 2]

While in the centre of the shield the sun's bright orb flashed light on the backs of his winged coursers; there too was the heavenly choir of stars, Pleiades and Hyades, to dazzle Hector's eyes and make him flee; and upon his gold-forged helm were sphinxes, bearing in their talons the prey of which the minstrels sing; on his breast-plate was lioness breathing flame, her eye upon Peirene's steed, in eagerness to rend it.

There too in murderous fray four-footed steeds were prancing, while oer their backs uprose dark clouds of dust. But he who led these warriors stout, was slain by wedding thee, malignant child of Tyndareus! Wherefore shall the gods of heaven one day send thee to thy doom, and I shall yet live to see the sword at thy throat, drinking its crimson tide.

[The **OLD MAN**, the former servant of Agamemnon, enters. **ELECTRA** presently appears at the door of the hut.]

OLD MAN
Where is the young princess, my mistress, Agamemnon's daughter, whom I nursed in days gone by? Oh! how steep is the approach to this house, a hard climb for these old wasted feet of mine! Still, to reach such friends as these, I must drag my bent old back and tottering knees up it. Ah, daughter!—for I see thee now at thy door,—lo! I have brought the this tender lamb from my own flock, having taken it from its dam, with garlands too and cheese straight from the press, and this flask of choice old wine with fragrant bouquet; 'tis small perhaps, but pour a cup thereof into some weaker drink, and it is a luscious draught. Let some one carry these gifts into the house for the guests; for I would fain wipe from my eyes the rising tears on this tattered cloak.

ELECTRA
Why stands the tear-drop in thine eye, old friend? Is it that my sorrows have been recalled to thee after an interval? or art thou bewailing the sad exile of Orestes, and my father's fate, whom thou didst once fondle in thy arms, in vain, alas! for thee and for thy friends?

OLD MAN
Ah yes! in vain; but still I could not bear to leave him thus; and so I added this to my journey that I sought his grave, and, falling thereupon, wept o'er its desolation; then did I open the wine-skin, my gift to thy guests, and poured a libation, and set myrtle-sprigs round the tomb. And lo! upon the grave itself I saw a black ram had been offered, and there was blood, not long poured forth, and severed locks of auburn hair. Much I wondered, my daughter, who had dared approach the tomb; certainly 'twas no Argive. Nay, thy brother may perchance have come by stealth, and going thither have done honour to

his father's wretched grave. Look at the hair, compare it with thy own, to see if the colour of these cut locks is the same; for children in whose veins runs the same father's blood have a close resemblance in many features.

ELECTRA
Old sir, thy words are unworthy of a wise man, if thou thinkest my own brave brother would have come to this land by stealth for fear of Aegisthus. In the next place, how should our hair correspond? His is the hair of a gallant youth trained up in manly sports, mine a woman's curled and combed; nay, that is a hopeless clue. Besides, thou couldst find many, whose hair is of the same colour, albeit not sprung from the same blood. No, maybe 'twas some stranger cut off his hair in pity at his tomb, or one that came to spy this land privily.

OLD MAN
Put thy foot in the print of his shoe and mark whether it correspond with thine, my child.

ELECTRA
How should the foot make any impression on stony ground? and if it did, the foot of brother and sister would not be the same in size, for man's is the larger.

OLD MAN
Hast thou no mark, in case thy brother should come, whereby to recognize the weaving of thy loom, the robe wherein I snatched him from death that day?

ELECTRA
Dost thou forget I was still a babe when Orestes left the country? and even if I had woven him a robe, how should he, a mere child then, be wearing the same now, unless our clothes and bodies grow together?

OLD MAN
Where are these guests? I fain would question them face to face about thy brother.

[As he speaks, **ORESTES** and **PYLADES** come out of the hut.]

ELECTRA
There they are, in haste to leave the house.

OLD MAN
Well born, it seems, but that may be a sham; for there be plenty such prove knaves. Still I give them greeting.

ORESTES
All hail, father! To which of thy friends, Electra, does this old relic of mortality belong?

ELECTRA
This is he who nursed my sire, sir stranger.

ORESTES
What! do I behold him who removed thy brother out of harm's way?

ELECTRA
Behold the man who saved his life; if, that is, he liveth still.

ORESTES
Ha! why does he look so hard at me, as if he were examining the bright device on silver coin? Is he finding in me a likeness to some other?

ELECTRA
Maybe he is glad to see in thee a companion of Orestes.

ORESTES
A man I love full well. But why is he walking round me?

ELECTRA
I, too, am watching his movements with amaze, sir stranger.

OLD MAN
My honoured mistress, my daughter Electra, return thanks to heaven,—

ELECTRA
For past or present favours? which?

OLD MAN
That thou hast found a treasured prize, which God is now revealing.

ELECTRA
Hear me invoke the gods. But what dost thou mean, old man?

OLD MAN
Behold before thee, my child, thy nearest and dearest.

ELECTRA I have long feared thou wert not in thy sound senses

OLD MAN Not in my sound senses, because I see thy brother?

ELECTRA
What mean'st thou, aged friend, by these astounding words?

OLD MAN
That I see Orestes, Agamemnon's son, before me.

ELECTRA
What mark dost see that I can trust?

OLD MAN
A scar along his brow, where he fell and cut himself one day in his father's home when chasing a fawn with thee.

ELECTRA
Is it possible? True; I see the mark of the fall.

OLD MAN
Dost hesitate then to embrace thy own dear brother?

ELECTRA
No! not any longer, old friend; for my soul is convinced by the tokens thou showest. O my brother, thou art come at last, and I embrace thee, little as I ever thought to.

ORESTES
And thee to my bosom at last I press.

ELECTRA
I never thought that it would happen.

ORESTES
All hope in me was also dead.

ELECTRA
Art thou really he?

ORESTES
Aye, thy one and only champion, if I can but safely draw to shore the cast I mean to throw; and I feel sure I shall; else must we cease to believe in gods, if wrong is to triumph o'er right.

CHORUS [singing]
At last, at last appears thy radiant dawn, O happy day! and as beacon to the city hast thou revealed the wanderer, who, long ago, poor boy! was exiled from his father's halls. Now, lady, comes our turn for victory, ushered in by some god. Raise hand and voice in prayer, beseech the gods that good fortune may attend thy brother's entry to the city.

ORESTES
Enough! sweet though the rapture of this greeting be, I must wait and return it hereafter. Do thou, old friend so timely met, tell me how I am to avenge me on my father's murderer, and on my mother, the partner in his guilty marriage. Have I still in Argos any band of kindly friends? or am I, like my fortunes, bankrupt altogether? With whom am I to league myself? by night or day shall I advance? point out a road for me to take against these foes of mine.

OLD MAN
My son, thou hast no friend now in thy hour of adversity. No! that is a piece of rare good luck, to find another share thy fortunes alike for better and for worse. Thou art of every friend completely reft, all hope is gone from thee; be sure of what I tell thee; on thy own arm and fortune art thou wholly thrown to win thy father's home and thy city.

ORESTES
What must I do to compass this result?

OLD MAN
Slay Thyestes' son and thy mother.

ORESTES
I came to win that victor's crown, but how can I attain it?

OLD MAN
Thou wouldst never achieve it if thou didst enter the walls.

ORESTES
Are they manned with guards and armed sentinels?

OLD MAN
Aye truly; for he is afraid of thee, and cannot sleep secure.

ORESTES
Well then, do thou next propose a scheme, old friend.

OLD MAN
Hear me a moment; an idea has just occurred to me.

ORESTES
May thy counsel prove good, and my perception keen!

OLD MAN
I saw Aegisthus, as I was slowly pacing hither—

ORESTES
I welcome thy words. Where was he?

OLD MAN
Not far from these fields, at his stables.

ORESTES
What was he doing? I see a gleam of hope after our helplessness.

OLD MAN
I thought he was preparing a feast for the Nymphs.

ORESTES
In return for the bringing up of children or in anticipation of a birth?

OLD MAN
All I know is this, he was preparing to sacrifice oxen.

ORESTES
How many were with him? or was he alone with his servants?

OLD MAN

There was no Argive there; only a band of his own followers.

ORESTES

Is it possible that any of them will recognize me, old man?

OLD MAN

They are only servants, and they have never even seen thee.

ORESTES

Will they support me, if I prevail?

OLD MAN

Yes, that is the way of slaves, luckily for thee.

ORESTES

On what pretext can I approach him?

OLD MAN

Go to some place where he will see thee as he sacrifices.

ORESTES

His estate is close to the road then, I suppose.

OLD MAN

Yes, and when he sees thee there, he will invite thee to the feast.

ORESTES

So help me God! He shall rue his invitation.

OLD MAN

After that, form thy own plan according to circumstances.

ORESTES

Good advice! But my mother, where is she?

OLD MAN

At Argos; but she will yet join her husband for the feast.

ORESTES

Why did she not come forth with him?

OLD MAN

From fear of the citizens' reproach she stayed behind.

ORESTES

I understand; she knows that the city suspects her.

OLD MAN
Just so; her wickedness makes her hated.

ORESTES
How shall I slay her and him together?

ELECTRA
Mine be the preparation of my mother's slaying!

ORESTES
Well, as for the other, fortune will favour us.

ELECTRA
Our old friend here must help us both.

OLD MAN
Aye, that will I; but wnat is thy scheme for slaying thy mother?

ELECTRA
Go, old man, and tell Clytemnestra from me that I have given birth to a son.

OLD MAN
Some time ago, or quite recently?

ELECTRA
Ten days ago, which are the days of my purification.

OLD MAN
Suppose it done; but how doth this help towards slaying thy mother?

ELECTRA
She will come, when she hears of my confinement.

OLD MAN
What! dost think she cares aught for thee, my child?

ELECTRA
Oh yes! she will weep no doubt over my child's low rank.

OLD MAN
Perhaps she may; but go back again to the point.

ELECTRA
Her death is certain, if she comes.

OLD MAN
In that case, let her come right up to the door of the house.

ELECTRA
Why then it were a little thing to turn her steps into the road to Hades' halls.

OLD MAN
Oh! to see this one day, then die!

ELECTRA
First of all, old friend, act as my brother's guide.

OLD MAN
To the place where Aegisthus is now sacrificing to the gods?

ELECTRA
Then go, find my mother and give her my message.

OLD MAN
Aye, that I will, so that she shall think the very words are thine.

ELECTRA [to **ORESTES**]
Thy work begins at once; thou hast drawn the first lot in the tragedy.

ORESTES
I will go, if some one will show me the way.

OLD MAN
I will myself conduct thee nothing loth.

ORESTES
O Zeus, god of my fathers, vanquisher of my foes, have pity on us, for a piteous lot has ours been.

ELECTRA
Oh! have pity on thy own descendants.

ORESTES
O Hera, mistress of Mycenae's altars, grant us the victory, if we are asking what is right.

ELECTRA
Yes, grant us vengeance on them for our father's death.

ORESTES
Thou too, my father, sent to the land of shades by wicked hands, and Earth, the queen of all, to whom I spread my suppliant palms, up and champion thy dear children. Come with all the dead to aid, all they who helped thee break the Phrygians' power, and all who hate ungodly crime. Dost hear me, father, victim of my mother's rage?

ELECTRA

Sure am I he heareth all; but 'tis time to part. For this cause too I bid thee strike Aegisthus down, because, if thou fall in the struggle and perish, I also die; no longer number me amongst the living; for I will stab myself with a two-edged sword. And now will I go indoors and make all ready there, for, if there come good news from thee, my house shall ring with women's cries of joy; but, if thou art slain, a different scene must then ensue. These are my instructions to thee.

ORESTES
I know my lesson well.

[**ORESTES**, **PYLADES**, **the OLD MAN**, and **ATTENDANTS**, depart.]

ELECTRA
Then show thyself a man. And you, my friends, signal to me by cries the certain issue of this fray. Myself will keep the sword ready in my grasp, for I will never accept defeat, and yield my body to my enemies to insult.

[**ELECTRA** goes into the hut.]

CHORUS [singing, strophe 1]
Still the story finds a place in time-honoured legends, how on day Pan, the steward of husbandry, came breathing dulcet music on his jointed pipe, and brought with him from its tender dam on Argive hills, a beauteous lamb with fleece of gold; then stood a herald high upon the rock and cried aloud, "Away to the place of assembly, ye folk of Mycenae! to behold the strange and awful sight vouchsafed to our blest rulers." Anon the dancers did obeisance to the family of Atreus;

[antistrophe 1]

The altar-steps of beaten gold were draped; and through that Argive town the altars blazed with fire; sweetly rose the lute's clear note, the handmaid of the Muse's song; and ballads fair were written on the golden lamb, saying that Thyestes had the luck; for he won the guilty love of the wife of Atreus, and carried off to his house the strange creature, and then coming before the assembled folk he declared to them that he had in his house that horned beast with fleece of gold.

[strophe 2]

In the self-same hour it was that Zeus changed the radiant courses of the stars, the light of the sun, and the joyous face of dawn, and drave his car athwart the western sky with fervent heat from heaven's fires, while northward fled the rain-clouds, and Ammon's strand grew parched and faint and void of dew, when it was robbed of heaven's genial showers.

[antistrophe 2]

'Tis said, though I can scarce believe it, the sun turned round his glowing throne of gold, to vex the sons of men by this change because of the quarrel amongst them. Still, tales of horror have their use in making men regard the gods; of whom thou hadst no thought, when thou slewest thy husband, thou mother of this noble pair.

LEADER OF THE CHORUS

Hark! my friends, did ye hear that noise, like to the rumbling of an earthquake, or am I the dupe of idle fancy? Hark! hark! once more that wind-borne sound swells loudly on mine ear. Electra! mistress mine! come forth from the house!

ELECTRA [rushing out]
What is it, good friends? how goes the day with us?

LEADER
I hear the cries of dying men; no more I know.

ELECTRA
I heard them too, far off, but still distinct.

LEADER
Yes, the sound came stealing from afar, but yet 'twas clear.

ELECTRA
Was it the groan of an Argive, or of my friends?

LEADER
I know not; for the cries are all confused.

ELECTRA
That word of thine is my death-warrant; why do I delay?

LEADER
Stay, till thou learn thy fate for certain.

ELECTRA
No, no; we are vanquished; where are our messengers?

LEADER
They will come in time; to slay a king is no light task.

[A **MESSENGER** enters in haste.]

MESSENGER
All hail! ye victors, maidens of Mycenae, to all Orestes' friends his triumph I announce; Aegisthus, the murderer of Agamemnon, lies weltering where he fell; return thanks to heaven.

ELECTRA
Who art thou? What proof dost thou give of this?

MESSENGER
Look at me, dost thou not recognize thy brother's servant?

ELECTRA

O best of friends! 'twas fear that prevented me from recognizing thee; now I know thee well. What sayst thou? Is my father's hateful murderer slain?

MESSENGER
He is; I repeat it since it is thy wish.

LEADER
Ye gods, and justice, whose eye is on all, at last art thou come.

ELECTRA
I fain would learn the way and means my brother took to slay Thyestes' son.

MESSENGER
After we had set out from this house, we struck into the broad highroad, and came to the place where was the far-famed King of Mycenae. Now he was walking in a garden well-watered, culling a wreath of tender myrtle-sprays for his head, and when he saw us, he called out, "All hail! strangers; who are ye? whence come ye? from what country?" To him Orestes answered, "We are from Thessaly, on our way to Alpheus' banks to sacrifice to Olympian Zeus." When Aegisthus heard that, he said, "Ye must be my guests to-day, and share the feast, for I am even now sacrificing to the Nymphs; and by rising with tomorrow's light ye will be just as far upon your journey; now let us go within." Therewith he caught us by the hand and led us by the way; refuse we could not; and when we were come to the house, he gave command: "Bring water for my guests to wash forthwith, that they may stand around the altar near the laver." But Orestes answered, "'Twas but now we purified ourselves and washed us clean in water from the river. So if we strangers are to join your citizens in sacrifice, we are ready, King Aegisthus, and will not refuse." So ended they their private conference. Meantime the servants, that composed their master's bodyguard, laid aside their weapons, and one and all were busied at their tasks. Some brought the bowl to catch the blood, others took up baskets, while others kindled fire and set cauldrons round about the altars, and the whole house rang. Then did thy mother's husband take the barley for sprinkling, and began casting it upon the hearth with these words, "Ye Nymphs, who dwell among the rocks, grant that I may often sacrifice with my wife, the daughter of Tyndareus, within my halls, as happily as now, and ruin seize my foes!" (whereby he meant Orestes and thyself] . But my master, lowering his voice, offered a different prayer, that he might regain his father's house. Next Aegisthus took from basket a long straight knife, and cutting off some of the calf's hair, laid it with his right hand on the sacred fire, and then cut its throat when the servants had lifted it upon their shoulders, and thus addressed thy brother; "Men declare that amongst the Thessalians this is counted honourable, to cut up a bull neatly and to manage steeds. So take the knife, sir stranger, and show us if rumour speaks true about the Thessalians." Thereon Orestes seized the Dorian knife of tempered steel and cast from his shoulders his graceful buckled robe; then choosing Pylades to help him in his task, he made the servants withdraw, and catching the calf by the hoof, proceeded to lay bare its white flesh, with arm outstretched, and he flayed the hide quicker than a runner ever finishes the two laps of the horses' race-course; next he laid the belly open, and Aegisthus took the entrails in his hands and carefully examined them. Now the liver had no lobe, while the portal vein leading to the gall-bladder portended dangerous attack on him who was observing it. Dark grows Aegisthus' brow, but my master asks, "Why so despondent, good sir?" Said he, "I fear treachery from a stranger. Agamemnon's son of all men most I hate, and he hates my house." But Orestes cried, "What! fear treachery from an exile! thou the ruler of the city? Ho! take this Dorian knife away and bring me a Thessalian cleaver, that we by sacrificial feast may learn the will of heaven; let me cleave the breast-bone." And he took the axe and cut it through. Now Aegisthus was examining the entrails, separating them in his hands, and as he was bending down,

thy brother rose on tiptoe and smote him on the spine, severing the bones of his back; and his body gave one convulsive shudder from head to foot and writhed in the death-agony. No sooner did his servants see it, than they rushed to arms, a host to fight with two; yet did Pylades and Orestes of their valiancy meet them with brandished spears. Then cried Orestes, "I am no foe that come against this city and my own servants, but I have avenged me on the murderer of my sire, I, ill-starred Orestes. Slay me not, my father's former thralls!" They, when they heard him speak, restrained their spears, and an old man, who had been in the family many a long year, recognized him. Forthwith they crown thy brother with a wreath, and utter shouts of joy. And lo! he is coming to show thee the head, not the Gorgon's, but the head of thy hated foe Aegisthus; his death today has paid in blood a bitter debt of blood.

CHORUS [singing]
Dear mistress, now with step as light as fawn join in the dance; lift high the nimble foot and be glad. Victory crowns thy brother; he hath won a fairer wreath than ever victor gained beside the streams of Alpheus; so raise a fair hymn to victory, the while I dance.

ELECTRA
O light of day! O bright careering sun! O earth! and night erewhile my only day; now may I open my eyes in freedom, for Aegisthus is dead, my father's murderer. Come friends, let me bring out whate'er my house contains to deck his head and wreath with crowns my conquering brother's brow.

CHORUS [singing]
Bring forth thy garlands for his head, and we will lead the dance the Muses love. Now shall the royal line, dear to us in days gone by, resume its sway o'er the realm, having laid low the usurper as he deserves. So let the shout go up, whose notes are those of joy.

[**ORESTES** and **PYLADES** enter, followed by **ATTENDANTS** who are bearing the body of **AEGISTHUS**.]

ELECTRA
Hail! glorious victor, Orestes, son of a sire who won the day 'neath Ilium's walls, accept this wreath to bind about the tresses of thy hair. Not in vain hast thou run thy course unto the goal and reached thy home again; no! but thou hast slain thy foe, Aegisthus, the murderer of our father. Thou too, O Pylades, trusty squire, whose training shows thy father's sterling worth, receive a garland from my hand, for thou no less than he hast a share in this emprise; and so I pray, good luck be thine for ever!

ORESTES
First recognize the gods, Electra, as being the authors of our fortune, and then praise me their minister and fate's. Yea, I come from having slain Aegisthus in very deed, no mere pretence; and to make thee the more certain of this, I am bringing thee his corpse, which, if thou wilt, expose for beasts to rend, or set it upon a stake for birds, the children of the air, to prey upon; for now is he thy slave, once called thy lord and master.

ELECTRA
I am ashamed to utter my wishes.

ORESTES
What is it? speak out, for thou art through the gates of fear.

ELECTRA

I am ashamed to flout the dead, for fear some spite assail me.

ORESTES
No one would blame thee for this.

ELECTRA
Our folk are hard to please, and love to blame.

ORESTES
Speak all thy mind, sister; for we entered on this feud with him on terms admitting not of truce.

ELECTRA
Enough!

[Turning to the corpse of **AEGISTHUS**]

With which of thy iniquities shall I begin my recital? With which shall I end it? To which allot a middle place? And yet I never ceased, as each day dawned, to rehearse the story I would tell thee to thy face, if ever I were freed from my old terrors; and now I am; so I will pay thee back with the abuse I fain had uttered to thee when alive. Thou wert my ruin, making me and my brother orphans, though we had never injured thee, and thou didst make a shameful marriage with my mother, having slain her lord who led the host of Hellas, though thyself didst never go to Troy. Such was thy folly, thou didst never dream that my mother would prove thy curse when thou didst marry her, though thou wert wronging my father's honour. Know this; whoso defiles his neighbour's wife, and afterward is forced to take her to himself, is a wretched wight, if he supposes she will be chaste as his wife, though she sinned against her former lord. Thine was a life most miserable, though thou didst pretend 'twas otherwise; well thou knewest how guilty thy marriage was, and my mother knew she had a villain for husband. Sinners both ye took each other's lot, she thy fortune, thou her curse. While everywhere in Argos thou-wouldst hear such phrases as, "that woman's husband," never "that man's wife." Yet 'tis shameful for the wife and not the man to rule the house; wherefore I loathe those children, who are called in the city not the sons of the man, their father, but of their mother. For if a man makes a great match above his rank, there is no talk of the husband but only of the wife. Herein lay thy grievous error, due to ignorance; thou thoughtest thyself some one, relying on thy wealth, but this is naught save to stay with us a space. 'Tis nature that stands fast, not wealth. For it, if it abide unchanged, exalts man's horn; but riches dishonestly acquired and in the hands of fools, soon take their flight, their blossom quickly shed. As for thy sins with women, I pass them by, 'tis not for maiden's lips to mention them, but I will shrewdly hint thereat. And then thy arrogance! because forsooth thou hadst a palace and some looks to boast. May I never have a husband with a girl's face, but one that bears him like a man! For the children of these latter cling to a life of arms, while those, who are so fair to see, do only serve to grace the dance. Away from me!

[Spurning the **CORPSE** with her foot]

Time has shown thy villainy, little as thou reckest of the forfeit thou hast paid for it. Let none suppose, though he have run the first stage of his course with joy, that he will get the better of justice, till he have reached the goal and ended his career.

LEADER OF THE CHORUS

Terrible alike his crime and your revenge; for mighty is the power of justice.

ORESTES
'Tis well. Carry his body within the house and hide it, sirrahs, that when my mother comes, she may not see his corpse before she is smitten herself.

[**PYLADES** and the **ATTENDANTS** take the body into the hut.]

ELECTRA
Hold! let us strike out another scheme.

ORESTES
How now? Are those allies from Mycenae whom I see?

ELECTRA
No, 'tis my mother, that bare me.

ORESTES
Full into the net she is rushing, oh, bravely!

ELECTRA
See how proudly she rides in her chariot and fine robes!

ORESTES
What must we do to our mother? Slay her?

ELECTRA
What! has pity seized thee at sight of her?

ORESTES
O God! how can I slay her that bare and suckled me?

ELECTRA
Slay her as she slew thy father and mine.

ORESTES
O Phoebus, how foolish was thy oracle—

ELECTRA
Where Apollo errs, who shall be wise?

ORESTES
In bidding me commit this crime—my mother's murder!

ELECTRA
How canst thou be hurt by avenging thy father?

ORESTES

Though pure before, I now shall carry into exile the stain of a mother's blood.

ELECTRA
Still, if thou avenge not thy father, thou wilt fail in thy duty.

ORESTES
And if I slay my mother, I must pay the penalty to her.

ELECTRA
And so must thou to him, if thou resign the avenging of our father.

ORESTES
Surely it was a fiend in the likeness of the god that ordered this!

ELECTRA
Seated on the holy tripod? I think not so.

ORESTES
I cannot believe this oracle was meant.

ELECTRA
Turn not coward! Cast not thy manliness away!

ORESTES
Am I to devise the same crafty scheme for her?

ELECTRA
The self-same death thou didst mete out to her lord Aegisthus.

ORESTES
I will go in; 'tis an awful task I undertake; an awful deed I have to do; still if it is Heaven's will, be it so; I loathe and yet I love the enterprise.

[As **ORESTES** withdraws into the hut, **CLYTEMNESTRA** enters in a chariot. Her **ATTENDANTS** are handmaidens attired in gorgeous apparel.]

CHORUS [singing]
Hail! Queen of Argos, daughter of Tyndareus, sister of those two noble sons of Zeus, who dwell in the flame-lit firmament amid the stars, whose guerdon high it is to save the sailor tossing on the sea. All hail! because of thy wealth and high prosperity, I do thee homage as I do the blessed gods. Now is the time, great queen, for us to pay our court unto thy fortunes.

CLYTEMNESTRA
Alight from the car, ye Trojan maids, and take my hand that I may step down from the chariot. With Trojan spoils the temples of the gods are decked, but I have obtained these maidens as a special gift from Troy, in return for my lost daughter, a trifling boon no doubt, but still an ornament to my house.

ELECTRA

And may not I, mother, take that highly-favoured hand of thine? I am a slave like them, an exile from my father's halls in this miserable abode.

CLYTEMNESTRA
See, my servants are here; trouble not on my account.

ELECTRA
Why, thou didst make me thy prisoner by robbing me of my home; like these I became a captive when my home was taken, an orphan all forlorn.

CLYTEMNESTRA
True; but thy father plotted so wickedly against those of his own kin whom least of all he should have treated so. Speak I must; albeit, when woman gets an evil reputation, there is a feeling of bitterness against all she says; unfairly indeed in my case, for it were only fair to hate after learning the circumstances, and seeing if the object deserves it; otherwise, why hate at all? Now Tyndareus bestowed me on thy father not that I or any children I might bear should be slain. Yet he went and took my daughter from our house to the fleet at Aulis, persuading me that Achilles was to wed her; and there he held her o'er the pyre, and cut Iphigenia's snowy throat. Had he slain her to save his city from capture, or to benefit his house, or to preserve his other children, a sacrifice of one for many, could have pardoned him. But, as it was, his reasons for murdering my child were these: the wantonness of Helen and her husband's folly in not punishing the traitress. Still, wronged as I was, my rage had not burst forth for this, nor would I have slain my lord, had he not returned to me with that frenzied maiden and made her his mistress, keeping at once two brides beneath the same roof. Women maybe are given to folly, I do not deny it; this granted, when a husband goes astray and sets aside his own true wife, she fain will follow his example and find another love; and then in our case hot abuse is heard, while the men, who are to blame for this, escape without a word. Again, suppose Menelaus had been secretly snatched from his home, should I have had to kill Orestes to save Menelaus, my sister's husband? How would thy father have endured this? Was he then to escape death for slaying what was mine, while I was to suffer at his hands? I slew him, turning, as my only course, to his enemies. For which of all thy father's friends would have joined me in his murder? Speak all that is in thy heart, and prove against me with all free speech, that thy father's death was not deserved.

ELECTRA
Justly urged! but thy justice is not free from shame; for in all things should every woman of sense yield to her husband. Whoso thinketh otherwise comes not within the scope of what I say. Remember, mother, those last words of thine, allowing me free utterance before thee.

CLYTEMNESTRA
Daughter, far from refusing it, I grant it again.

ELECTRA
Thou wilt not, when thou hearest, wreak thy vengeance on me?

CLYTEMNESTRA
No, indeed; I shall welcome thy opinion.

ELECTRA

Then will I speak, and this shall be the prelude of my speech: Ah, mother mine! would thou hadst had a better heart; for though thy beauty and Helen's win you praises well deserved, yet are ye akin in nature, pair of wantons, unworthy of Castor. She was carried off, 'tis true, but her fall was voluntary: and thou hast slain the bravest soul in Hellas, excusing thyself on the ground that thou didst kill a husband to avenge a daughter; the world does not know thee so well as I do, thou who before ever thy daughter's death was decided, yea, soon as thy lord had started from his home, wert combing thy golden tresses at thy mirror. That wife who, when her lord is gone from home, sets to beautifying herself, strike off from virtue's list; for she has no need to carry her beauty abroad, save she is seeking some mischief. Of all the wives in Hellas thou wert the only one I know who wert overjoyed when Troy's star was in the ascendant, while, if it set, thy brow was clouded, since thou hadst no wish that Agamemnon should return from Troy. And yet thou couldst have played a virtuous part to thy own glory. The husband thou hadst was no whit inferior to Aegisthus, for he it was whom Hellas chose to be her captain. And when thy sister Helen wrought that deed of shame, thou couldst have won thyself great glory, for vice is a warning and calls attention to virtue. If, as thou allegest, my father slew thy daughter, what is the wrong I and my brother have done thee? How was it thou didst not bestow on us our father's halls after thy husband's death, instead of bartering them to buy a paramour? Again, thy husband is not exiled for thy son's sake, nor is he slain to avenge my death, although by him this life is quenched twice as much as e'er my sister's was; so if murder is to succeed murder in requital, I and thy son Orestes must slay thee to avenge our father; if that was just, why so is this. Whoso fixes his gaze on wealth or noble birth and weds a wicked woman, is a fool; better is a humble partner in his home, if she be virtuous, than a proud one.

LEADER OF THE CHORUS
Chance rules the marriages of women; some I see turn out well, others ill amongst mankind.

CLYTEMNESTRA
Daughter, 'twas ever thy nature to love thy father. This too one finds; some sons cling to their father, others have a deeper affection for their mother. I will forgive thee, for myself am not so exceeding glad at the deed that I have done, my child. But thou,—why thus unwashed and clad in foul attire, now that the days of thy lying-in are accomplished? Ah me, for my sorry schemes! I have goaded my husband into anger more than e'er I should have done.

ELECTRA
Thy sorrow comes too late; the hour of remedy has gone from thee; my father is dead. Yet why not recall that exile, thy own wandering son?

CLYTEMNESTRA
I am afraid; 'tis my interest, not his that I regard. For they say he is wroth for his father's murder.

ELECTRA
Why, then, dost thou encourage thy husband's bitterness against us?

CLYTEMNESTRA
'Tis his way; thou too hast a stubborn nature.

ELECTRA
Because I am grieved; yet will I check my spirit.

CLYTEMNESTRA

I promise then he shall no longer oppress thee.

ELECTRA

From living in my home he grows too proud.

CLYTEMNESTRA

Now there! 'tis thou that art fanning the quarrel into new life.

ELECTRA

I say no more; my dread of him is even what it is.

CLYTEMNESTRA

Peace! Enough of this. Why didst thou summon me, my child?

ELECTRA

Thou hast heard, I suppose, of my confinement; for this I pray thee, since I know not how, offer the customary sacrifice on the tenth day after birth, for I am a novice herein, never having had a child before.

CLYTEMNESTRA

This is work for another, even for her who delivered thee.

ELECTRA

I was all alone in my travail and at the babe's birth.

CLYTEMNESTRA

Dost live so far from neighbours?

ELECTRA

No one cares to make the poor his friends.

CLYTEMNESTRA

Well, I will go to offer to the gods a sacrifice for the child's completion of the days; and when I have done thee this service, I will seek the field where my husband is sacrificing to the Nymphs. Take this chariot hence, my servants, and tie the horses to the stalls; and when ye think that I have finished my offering to the gods, attend me, for I must likewise pleasure my lord.

[She goes into the hut.]

ELECTRA

Enter our humble cottage; but, prithee, take care that my smoke grimed walls soil not thy robes; now wilt thou offer to the gods a fitting sacrifice. There stands the basket ready, and the knife is sharpened, the same that slew the bull, by whose side thou soon wilt lie a corpse; and thou shalt be his bride in Hades' halls whose wife thou wast on earth. This is the boon I will grant thee, while thou shalt pay me for my father's blood.

[**ELECTRA** follows her into the hut.]

CHORUS [chanting, strophe]
Misery is changing sides; the breeze veers round, and now blows fair upon my house. The day is past when my chief fell murdered in his bath, and the roof and the very stones of the walls rang with this his cry: "O cruel wife, why art thou murdering me on my return to my dear country after ten long years?"

[antistrophe]

The tide is turning, and justice that pursues the faithless wife is drawing within its grasp the murderess, who slew her hapless lord, when he came home at last to these towering Cyclopean walls,—aye, with her own hand she smote him with the sharpened steel, herself the axe uplifting. Unhappy husband! whate'er the curse that possessed that wretched woman. Like a lioness of the hills that rangeth through the woodland for her prey, she wrought the deed.

CLYTEMNESTRA [within]
O my children, by Heaven I pray ye spare your mother.

CHORUS [chanting]
Dost hear her cries within the house?

CLYTEMNESTRA
O God! ah me!

CHORUS [chanting]
I too bewail thee, dying by thy children's hands. God deals out His justice in His good time. A cruel fate is thine, unhappy one; yet didst thou sin in murdering thy lord.

[**ORESTES** and **ELECTRA** come out of the hut, followed by attendants who are carrying the two corpses. The following lines between **ELECTRA**, **ORESTES** and the **CHORUS** are chanted.]

But lo! from the house they come, dabbled in their mother's fresh-spilt gore, their triumph proving the piteous butchery. There is not nor ever has been a race more wretched than the line of Tantalus.

ORESTES
O Earth, and Zeus whose eye is over all! behold this foul deed of blood, these two corpses lying here that I have slain in vengeance for my sufferings.

ELECTRA
Tears are all too weak for this, brother; and I am the guilty cause. Ah, woe is me! How hot my fury burned against the mother that bare me!

ORESTES
Alas! for thy lot, O mother mine! A piteous, piteous doom, aye, worse than that, hast thou incurred at children's hands! Yet justly hast thou paid forfeit for our father's blood. Ah, Phoebus! thine was the voice that praised this vengeance; thou it is that hast brought these hideous scenes to light, and caused this deed of blood. To what city can I go henceforth? what friend, what man of any piety will bear the sight of a mother's murderer like me?

ELECTRA
Ah me! alas! and whither can I go? What share have I henceforth in dance or marriage rite? What husband will accept me as his bride?

ORESTES
Again thy fancy changes with the wind; for now thou thinkest aright, though not so formerly; an awful deed didst thou urge thy brother against his will to commit, dear sister. Oh! didst thou see how the poor victim threw open her robe and showed her bosom as smote her, sinking on her knees, poor wretch? And her hair I—

ELECTRA
Full well I know the agony through which thou didst pass at hearing thy own mother's bitter cry.

ORESTES
Ah yes! she laid her band upon my chin, and cried aloud, "My child, I entreat thee!" and she clung about my neck, so that I let fall the sword.

ELECTRA
O my poor mother! How didst thou endure to see her breathe her last before thy eyes?

ORESTES
I threw my mantle o'er them and began the sacrifice by plunging the sword into my mother's throat.

ELECTRA
Yet 'twas I that urged thee on, yea, and likewise grasped the steel. Oh! I have done an awful deed.

ORESTES
Oh! take and hide our mother's corpse beneath a pall, and close her gaping wound.

[Turning to the **CORPSE**]

Ah! thy murderers were thine own children.

ELECTRA [covering the **CORPSE**]
There! thou corpse both loved and loathed; still o'er thee I cast robe, to end the grievous troubles of our house.

CHORUS
See! where o'er the roof-top spirits are appearing, or gods maybe from heaven, for this is not a road that mortals tread. Why come they thus where mortal eyes can see them clearly?

[THE **DIOSCURI** appear from above.]

DIOSCURI
Hearken, son of Agamemnon. We, the twin sons of Zeus, thy mother's sisters, call thee, even Castor and his brother Polydeuces. 'Tis but now we have reached Argos after stilling the fury of the sea for mariners, having seen the slaying of our sister, thy mother. She hath received her just reward, but thine is no righteous act, and Phoebus—but no! he is my king, my lips are sealed—is Phoebus still, albeit the

oracle he gave thee was no great proof of his wsdom. But we must acquiesce herein. Henceforth must thou follow what Zeus and destiny ordain for thee. On Pylades bestow Electra for his wife to take unto his home; do thou leave Argos, for after thy mother's murder thou mayst not set foot in the city. And those grim goddesses of doom, that glare like savage hounds, will drive thee mad and chase thee to and fro; but go thou to Athens and make thy prayer to the holy image of Pallas, for she will close their fierce serpents' mouths, so that they touch thee not, holding o'er thy head her aegis with the Gorgon's head. A hill there is, to Ares sacred, where first the gods in conclave sat to decide the law of blood, in the day that savage Ares slew Halirrothius, son of the ocean-king, in anger for the violence he offered to his daughter's honour; from that time all decisions given there are most holy and have heaven's sanction. There must thou have this murder tried; and if equal votes are given, they shall save thee from death in the decision, for Loxias will take the blame upon himself, since it was his oracle that advised thy mother's murder. And this shall be the law for all posterity; in every trial the accused shall win his case if the votes are equal. Then shall those dread goddesses, stricken with grief at this, vanish into a cleft of the earth close to the hill, revered by men henceforth as a place for holy oracles; whilst thou must settle in a city of Arcadia on the banks of the river Alpheus near the shrine of Lycaean Apollo, and the city shall be called after thy name. To thee I say this. As for the corpse of Aegisthus, the citizens of Argos must give it burial; but Menelaus, who has just arrived at Nauplia from the sack of Troy, shall bury the, mother, Helen helping him; for she hath come from her sojourn in Egypt in the halls of Proteus, and hath never been to Troy; but Zeus, to stir up strife and bloodshed in the world, sent forth a phantom of Helen to Ilium. Now let Pylades take his maiden wife and bear her to his home in Achaea; also he must conduct thy so-called kinsman to the land of Phocis, and there reward him well. But go thyself along the narrow Isthmus, and seek Cecropia's happy home. For once thou hast fulfilled the doom appointed for this murder, thou shalt be blest and free from all thy troubles.

[The remaining lines of the play are chanted.]

CHORUS
Ye sons of Zeus, may we draw near to speak with you?

DIOSCURI
Ye may, since ye are not polluted by this murder.

ORESTES
May I too share your converse, of Tyndareus?

DIOSCURI
Thou too! for to Phoebus will I ascribe this deed of blood.

CHORUS
How was it that ye, the brothers of the murdered woman, gods too, did not ward the doom-goddesses from her roof?

DIOSCURI
'Twas fate that brought resistless doom to her, and that thoughtless oracle that Phoebus gave.

ELECTRA
But why did the god, and wherefore did his oracles make me my mother's murderer?

DIOSCURI

A share in the deed, a share in its doom; one ancestral curse hath ruined both of you.

ORESTES

Ah, sister mine! at last I see thee again only to be robbed in moment of thy dear love; I must leave thee, and by thee be left.

DIOSCURI

Hers are a husband and a home; her only suffering this, that she is quitting Argos.

ORESTES

Yet what could call forth deeper grief than exile from one's fatherland? I must leave my father's house, and at a stranger's bar he sentenced for my mother's blood.

DIOSCURI

Be of good cheer; go to the holy town of Pallas; keep a stout heart only.

ELECTRA

O my brother, best and dearest! clasp me to thy breast; for now is the curse of our mother's blood cutting us off from the home of our fathers.

ORESTES

Throw thy arms in close embrace about me. Oh! weep as o'er my grave when I am dead.

DIOSCURI

Ah me, that bitter cry makes even gods shudder to hear. Yea, for in my breast and in every heavenly being's dwells pity for the sorrows of mankind.

ORESTES

Never to see thee more!

ELECTRA

Never again to stand within thy sight!

ORESTES

This is my last good-bye to thee.

ELECTRA

Farewell, farewell, my city! and ye my fellow-countrywomen, long farewell to you!

ORESTES

Art thou going already, truest of thy sex?

ELECTRA

I go, the tear-drop dimming my tender eyes.

ORESTES

Go, Pylades, and be happy; take and wed Electra.

DIOSCURI

Their only thoughts will be their marriage; but haste thee to Athens, seeking to escape these hounds of hell, for they are on thy track in fearful wise, swart monsters, with snakes for hands, who reap a harvest of man's agony. But we twain must haste away o'er the Sicilian main to save the seaman's ship. Yet as we fly through heaven's expanse we help not the wicked; but whoso in his life loves piety and justice, all such we free from troublous toils and save. Wherefore let no man be minded to act unjustly, or with men foresworn set sail; such the warning I, a god, to mortals give.

[THE **DIOSCURI** vanish.]

CHORUS

Farewell! truly that mortal's is a happy lot, who can thus fare, unafflicted by any woe.

Euripides – A Short Biography

Euripides is rightly lauded as one of the great dramatists of all time. In his lifetime, he wrote over 90 plays and although only 18 have survived they reveal the scope and reach of his genius.

Euripides is identified with many theatrical innovations that have influenced drama all the way down to modern times, especially in the representation of traditional, mythical heroes as ordinary people in extraordinary circumstances. This new approach led him to pioneer developments that later writers would adapt to comedy. Yet he also became "the most tragic of poets", focusing on the inner lives and motives of his characters in a way previously unknown. He was "the creator of...that cage which is the theatre of Shakespeare's Othello, Racine's Phèdre, of Ibsen and Strindberg," in which "...imprisoned men and women destroy each other by the intensity of their loves and hates", and yet he was also the literary ancestor of comic dramatists as diverse as Menander and George Bernard Shaw.

As would be expected from a life lived 2,500 years ago, details of it are few and far between. Accounts of his life, written down the ages, do exist but whether much is reliable or surmised is open to debate.

Most accounts agree that he was born on Salamis Island around 480 BC, to mother Cleito and father Mnesarchus, a retailer who lived in a village near Athens. Upon the receipt of an oracle saying that his son was fated to win "crowns of victory", Mnesarchus insisted that the boy should train for a career in athletics.

His education was not only confined to athletics: he also studied painting and philosophy under the masters Prodicus and Anaxagoras.

However, what became quickly very clear was that athletics was not to be his way to win crowns of victory. Euripides had been lucky enough to have been born in the era as the other two masters of Greek Tragedy; Sophocles and Æschylus. It was in their footsteps that he was destined to follow.

His first play was performed some thirteen years after the first of Socrates plays and a mere three years after Æschylus had written his classic The Oristria.

Theatre was becoming a very important part of the Greek culture. The Dionysia, held annually, was the most important festival of theatre and second only to the fore-runner of the Olympic games, the Panathenia, held every four years, in its appeal. It was a large festival in ancient Athens in honor of the god Dionysus, the central events of which were the theatrical performances of dramatic tragedies and, from 487 BC, comedies. The Dionysia actually consisted of two related festivals, the Rural Dionysia and the City Dionysia, which took place in different parts of the year.

Euripides first competed in the City Dionysia, in 455 BC, one year after the death of Æschylus, and, incredibly, it was not until 441 BC that he won first prize. His final competition in Athens was in 408 BC. However, The Bacchae and Iphigenia in Aulis were performed after his death in 405 BC and first prize was awarded posthumously. Altogether his plays won first prize only five times.

His plays, and those of Æschylus and Sophocles, indicate a difference in outlook between the three men, most easily explained as a generational gap, although with three great talents overlapping the driving forces may have pushed individual styles onwards perhaps faster than they may otherwise have done. Æschylus still looked back to the archaic period, Sophocles was in transition between periods, and Euripides was fully bonded with the new spirit of the classical age. When Euripides' plays are sequenced in time, they also show a developing pattern:

An early period of high tragedy (Medea, Hippolytus)
A patriotic period at the outset of the Peloponnesian War (Children of Hercules, Suppliants)
A middle period of disillusionment at the senselessness of war (Hecuba, Women of Troy)
An escapist period with a focus on romantic intrigue (Ion, Iphigenia in Tauris, Helen)
A final period of tragic despair (Orestes, Phoenician Women, Bacchae)

However, with over three quarters of his plays lost it is difficult to be certain as to whether the other works would also represent this development (e.g., Iphigenia at Aulis is dated with the 'despairing' Bacchae, yet it contains elements that became typical of New Comedy). In the Bacchae, he restores the chorus and messenger speech to their traditional role in the tragic plot, and the play appears to be the culmination of a regressive or archaizing tendency in his later works.

In one of his earliest surviving plays, Medea, includes a speech that he seems to have written in defence of himself as an intellectual ahead of his time, and to further challenge the times he has put the words in the mouth of the play's heroine:

"If you introduce new, intelligent ideas to fools, you will be thought frivolous, not intelligent. On the other hand, if you do get a reputation for surpassing those who are supposed to be intellectually sophisticated, you will seem to be a thorn in the city's flesh. This is what has happened to me." — Medea.

As we know Athenian tragedies during Euripides' lifetime were a public contest between playwrights. The state funded that contest and awarded prizes to the winners. The language was spoken and sung verse, the performance area included a circular floor or orchestra where the chorus could dance, a space for actors (usually three speaking actors in Euripides' time), a backdrop or skene and some special effects: an ekkyklema (used to bring the skene's "indoors" outdoors) and a mechane (used to lift actors in the air, as in deus ex machina). With the introduction of the third actor (an innovation attributed to Sophocles), acting also began to be regarded as a skill to be rewarded with prizes, requiring a long apprenticeship in the chorus. Euripides and other playwrights accordingly composed more and more arias for accomplished actors to sing and this tendency becomes more marked in his later plays: tragedy for him was a living and ever-changing genre.

Accounts by the famed comic poet, Aristophanes, characterise Euripides as a spokesman for destructive, new ideas, that mirror or help to bring about declining standards in both society and tragedy. However, 5th century tragedy was a social gathering for "carrying out quite publicly the maintenance and development of mental infrastructure" and it offered spectators a "platform for an utterly unique form of institutionalized discussion". A dramatist's role was not just to entertain but also to educate his fellow citizens—he was expected to have a message. Clearly this use of drama to democratize discussion was a very useful tool for all sides. Traditional myth provided the subject matter but the dramatist was meant to be innovative so as to sustain interest, which led to novel characterization of heroic figures and to use the mythical past to talk about present issues. The difference between Euripides and his older colleagues was, again, one of degree: his characters talked about the present more controversially and more pointedly than did those of Æschylus and Sophocles, sometimes even challenging the democratic order. Thus, for example, Odysseus is represented in Hecuba as "agile-minded, sweet-talking, demos-pleasing" i.e., a type of the war-time demagogues that were active in Athens during the Peloponnesian War. His concept is pleasingly simple. He retains the old stories and myths as well as the great names of the past and places them in the lives of contemporary Athenians thereby immediately help the audience understand it from the point of view of their own lives.

As mouthpieces for contemporary issues, they all seem to have had at least an elementary course in public speaking. Sometimes the dialogue often contrasts so strongly with the mythical and heroic setting, it looks as if Euripides aimed at parody, as for example in The Trojan Women, where the heroine's rationalized prayer provokes comment from Menelaus:

Hecuba:...O Zeus, whether you are the Law of Necessity in nature, or the Law of Reason in man, hear my prayers. You are everywhere, pursuing your noiseless path, ordering the affairs of mortals according to justice.

Menelaus: What's this? You are starting a new fashion in prayer.

Athenian citizens were familiar with rhetoric in the assembly and law courts, and some scholars believe that Euripides was more interested in his characters as speakers with cases to argue than as characters with lifelike personalities. They are self-conscious about speaking formally and their rhetoric is shown to be flawed, as if Euripides was exploring the problematical nature of language and communication: "For speech points in three different directions at once, to the speaker, to the person addressed, to the features in the world it describes, and each of these directions can be felt as skewed". Thus in the example above, Hecuba presents herself as a sophisticated intellectual describing a rationalised cosmos yet the speech is ill-matched to her audience, Menelaus (an unsophisticated listener), and soon it is found not to suit the cosmos either (her infant grandson is brutally murdered by the victorious Greeks).

Æschylus and Sophocles were innovative, but Euripides could move easily between tragic, comic, romantic and political effects, a versatility that appears in individual plays and also over the course of his career. Potential for comedy lay in his use of 'contemporary' characters, in his sophisticated tone, his relatively informal Greek, and his ingenious use of plots centered on motifs that later became standard, such as the 'recognition scene'. Other tragedians also used recognition scenes but they were heroic in emphasis, as in Æschylus's The Libation Bearers, which Euripides parodied with his mundane treatment of it in Electra (Euripides was unique among the tragedians in incorporating theatrical criticism in his plays). Traditional myth, with its exotic settings, heroic adventures and epic battles, offered potential for romantic melodrama as well as for political comments on a war theme, so that his plays are an extraordinary mix of elements. The Trojan Women for example is a powerfully disturbing play on the theme of war's horrors, apparently critical of Athenian imperialism (it was composed in the aftermath of the Melian massacre and during the preparations for the Sicilian Expedition) yet it features the comic exchange between Menelaus and Hecuba quoted above and the chorus considers Athens, the "blessed land of Theus", to be a desirable refuge—such complexity and ambiguity are typical both of his "patriotic" and "anti-war" plays.

Tragic poets in the 5th century competed against one another at the City Dionysia, each with a tetralogy consisting of three tragedies and a satyr-play. The few extant fragments of satyr-plays attributed to Æschylus and Sophocles indicate that these were a loosely structured, simple and jovial form of entertainment. However, in Cyclops (the only complete Euripides satyr-play that survives) the entertainment is structured more like a tragedy and introduced a note of critical irony typical of his other work. His genre-bending inventiveness is shown above all in Alcestis, a blend of tragic and satyric elements. This fourth play in his tetralogy for 438 BC (i.e., it occupied the position conventionally reserved for satyr-plays) is a "tragedy" that features Heracles as a satyric hero in conventional satyr-play scenes, involving an arrival, a banquet, a victory over an ogre (in this case, Death), a happy ending, a feast and a departure to new adventures.

Euripides was also a great lyric poet. In Medea, for example, he composed for his city, Athens, "the noblest of her songs of praise". His lyric skills however are not just confined to individual poems: "A play of Euripides is a musical whole....one song echoes motifs from the preceding song, while introducing new ones."

Much of his life and his whole career coincided with the struggle between Athens and Sparta for hegemony in Greece but he didn't live to see the final defeat of his city.

It is said that he died in Macedonia after being attacked by the Molossian hounds of King Archelaus and that his cenotaph near Piraeus was struck by lightning—signs of his unique powers, whether for good or ill. In an account by Plutarch, the complete failure of the Sicilian expedition led Athenians to trade renditions of Euripides' lyrics to their enemies in return for food and drink (Life of Nicias 29). Plutarch is the source also for the story that the victorious Spartan generals, having planned the demolition of Athens and the enslavement of its people, grew merciful after being entertained at a banquet by lyrics from Euripides' play Electra: "they felt that it would be a barbarous act to annihilate a city which produced such men" (Life of Lysander).

In The Frogs, composed after Euripides and Æschylus were both dead, Aristophanes imagines the god Dionysus venturing down to Hades in search of a good poet to bring back to Athens. After a debate between the two deceased bards, the god brings Æschylus back to life as more useful to Athens on account of his wisdom, rejecting Euripides as merely clever. Such comic 'evidence' suggests that Athenians admired Euripides even while they mistrusted his intellectualism, at least during the long war with Sparta.

Euripides had a famous library—one of the first to be privately collected. Although he lived most of his life in the midst of the cultured society of Athens, and was in some respects a leader in it, he grew bitter and despondent over the fierce rivalries and greedy ambitions which ran through the city. He loved the seclusion of his house at Salamis, where it was said that he composed his dramas in a cave.

Euripides fell out of favour with his fellow Athenian citizens and retired to the court of Archelaus, king of Macedon, who treated him with consideration and affection.

At his death, in around 406BC, he was mourned by the king, who, refusing the request of the Athenians that his remains be carried back to the Greek city, buried him with much splendor within his own dominions. His tomb was placed at the confluence of two streams, near Arethusa in Macedonia, and a cenotaph was built to his memory on the road from Athens towards the Piraeus.

Euripides – A Concise Bibliography

Alcestis (438 BC)
Medea (431 BC)
Heracleidae (c. 430 BC)
Hippolytus (428 BC)
Andromache (c. 425 BC)
Hecuba (c. 424 BC)
The Suppliants (c. 423 BC)
Electra (c. 420 BC)
Heracles (c. 416 BC)
The Trojan Women (c. 415 BC)
Iphigenia in Tauris (c. 414 BC)
Ion (c. 414 BC)
Helen (c. 412 BC)
Phoenician Women (c. 410 BC)
Orestes (c.408 BC)
Bacchae (405 BC)
Iphigenia at Aulis (405 BC)
Rhesus
Cyclops

Lost and Fragmentary Plays (Dated)

Peliades (455 BC)
Telephus (438 BC with Alcestis)
Alcmaeon in Psophis (438 BC with Alcestis)
Cretan Women (438 with Alcestis)
Cretans (c. 435 BC)
Philoctetes (431 BC with Medea)
Dictys (431 BC with Medea)
Theristai (satyr play, 431 BC with Medea)
Stheneboea (before 429 BC)
Bellerophon (c. 430 BC)
Cresphontes (ca. 425 BC)
Erechtheus (422 BC)

Phaethon (c. 420 BC)
Wise Melanippe (c. 420 BC)
Alexandros (415 BC with Trojan Women)
Palamedes (415 BC with Trojan Women)
Sisyphus (satyr play, 415 BC with Trojan Women)
Captive Melanippe (c. 412 BC)
Andromeda (412 BC with Helen)
Antiope (c. 410 BC)
Archelaus (c. 410 BC)
Hypsipyle (c. 410 BC)
Alcmaeon in Corinth (c. 405 BC) Won first prize as part of a trilogy with The Bacchae and Iphigenia in Aulis.

Lost and Fragmentary Plays (Not Dated)

Aegeus
Aeolus
Alcmene
Alope, or Cercyon
Antigone
Auge
Autolycus
Busiris
Cadmus
Chrysippus
Danae
Epeius
Eurystheus
Hippolytus Veiled
Ino
Ixion
Lamia
Licymnius
Meleager
Mysians
Oedipus
Oeneus
Oenomaus
Peirithous
Peleus
Phoenix
Phrixus
Pleisthenes
Polyidus
Protesilaus
Reapers
Rhadamanthys

www.ingramcontent.com/pod-product-compliance
Lightning Source LLC
Chambersburg PA
CBHW060101050426
42448CB00011B/2573